ORACLE
OF THE HEART
WHISPERINGS OF WISDOM
FOR DAILY REFLECTION

LUJAN MATUS

Disclaimer

www.parallelperception.com

In gratitude

To Mizpah, my beautiful wife,

I love you so dearly.

Heartfelt thanks to Maka for gathering notes

during workshops so we could retrieve

the majority of these sayings.

Thank you to Naomi for your loving devotion

all these years, I love you heaps.

www.parallelperception.com

Acknowledgements

Editing, formatting, cover art,

design layout and synopsis

by Naomi Jean.

How To Consult
The Oracle of the Heart

Open up these pages randomly
and discover yourself within their meanings.

The purpose of an oracle is to openly reveal information within the reservoirs of one's own inspiration. Trust yourself to respond to the mechanisms of no mind that will arise through the

www.parallelperception.com

process of your heartfelt feelings coming upon you. Engaging within this reflective mirror will unveil the clarity of your life path as it continually unfolds within your daily practices of sincerity. The Oracle can be consulted diligently on a regular basis or whenever you feel the need to explore.

Whatever you gaze at gazes back at you.

Within this exchange

you will always find yourself inwardly reflected. This is

your heart of hearts,

calling and responding to itself.

When you listen to the song of a beautiful bird

- when you truly listen -

you hear yourself singing.

The truest teacher we have

is the time we spend on this planet

and how we utilize that time.

There you have your teacher:

Your living circumstances

and your own silent reservoirs of energy.

A pure heart and an empty mind

will allow things to be seen clearly

in comparison to one's power, intertwined

with the momentum of one's life path.

One has to be free

of the idea that one has seen.

Be at a point that one does not know anything

and allow yourself to come upon

everything you need to know.

You must wait for the feeling

of your inner voice to arrive.

You must wait for imagery

to give you realization.

These insights will bring knowledge

that is filled with wisdom and power.

We live our truth through momentary realizations,

which cause a necessary ripple

within our living matrix

that will lead to a beneficial outcome.

When one watches what one cannot see and hears

what one cannot hear, one starts to feel.

Go very deeply into non-doing and do not get caught
in what others want to anchor you to. Relax before
their resistance and make a choice of what to do or
what not to do. Be neutral.

Be kind and comforting in the morning.

Be calm and tranquil in the evening.

Be mindful of the moments in between, for they define

the contours of your reality. This is the foundation for

true and loving communion.

www.parallelperception.com

No matter where you go,

you always arrive exactly where you are.

You can travel clear across the planet

but you can never escape yourself.

Believing something completely becomes a bias,

so believe without believing.

Go beyond the point of seeking confirmation.

www.parallelperception.com

Let go of your mind and be empty.

Be without being and do without doing.

The holographic universe is at your disposal.

All you have to do is clear out

the socially determined conditioning

that has been impressed upon you.

Realize that you are nothing

and you will become everything.

Defining a boundary

around one's sacred space

is natural self-preservation.

We are constantly being geared into a position to focus on what's unnecessary. Our feelings have a tendency under the programming to go to places and emotions that should not even be there. Unnecessary attentions become a way to slow us down or lower our frequencies, which takes us further away from our Heart Path.

You are a light being waking up

to the dimensionality of our universe

and to our capacity to be interlinked

on such a massive level that, when it happens, energy

and information rushes in,

and the photonic intensity of your heart center floods

your third eye. Thus you will gain access

to that which was unrealized previously.

Do not engage with things

that would injure one's heart.

Defending oneself is actually a form of harm,

let it happen and do not do what they do.

Learn to be neutral and not respond

to your own internal resistances.

When you encounter others you look within yourself,

for you are them and they become you. This is the

union that we have forgotten.

We have been separated from our eternal nature

by our belief in duality.

Even if we simply gaze at one another

for the slightest moment, our compartments become

combined. Every interaction entails a synthesis

of our subtle fields of perception.

As personal perimeters are being breached,

navigate storms with truths.

Crisis is an exceptional case that requires our full strength to stand up for ourselves. We can only try our best to be centered and see through those tricks that our environment is applying.

It is never too late.

We awaken to the true relevance of the moment

by connecting to something

much greater than ourselves.

www.parallelperception.com

If enough of us live within our integrity, it will have a shattering effect on the imprisoning principles of the general awareness of humanity.

What happens will be a cathartic transformation, in terms of the current social paradigm shifting away from what we are doing and toward what we are actually meant to be doing.

Let go of all your expectations,

for there may be something else expected of you.

Adaptation without corruption

is the key to personal power.

We all know when compromise happens.

The love you withold

is the pain that you carry.

Ralph Waldo Emerson

No need to decide that you need to do something,

simply make the change.

www.parallelperception.com

One has to be empty and abandoned in order to be
capable of directing one's own path.

www.parallelperception.com

If there's no conviction that you already are,

you will always be searching.

The world is a mystery,

yet that mystery unfolds itself

if we are open enough to receive.

Love is a gateway and the only one that matters.

The simple things that you do

every day with devotion

will reveal the world around you.

To listen to the unspoken

is to hear what can't be heard.

Reduction maps you

to the most powerful point.

Keep a sustained awareness of other people

but do not judge them.

Be both suspicious and kind at the same time.

We must not ignore,

neither should we acknowledge.

Always be aware that reducing oneself

is more important than your rational relevance.

Do not wrestle with anyone,

learn to overcome yourself first.

As we press

upon one another

with our intentions,

from our hearts fly

luminous butterflies,

that intermingle

and crossover

to be absorbed.

In abeyance

our hearts await.

43

Never forget what you are

meant to remember.

The magic moment when communion takes place is

beyond the capacities of what

one's mind can understand.

Life is a journey within.

Wisdom reveals itself through the act

of watching what you can't see,

listening to what you can't hear

and feeling that which can't be touched.

Allow your devotion to become

part and parcel of your whole being.

There's no choosing

as everything is chosen for us.

An old Cherokee once told his grandson: "My son, inside us all there is a battle between two wolves. One is Evil. It is anger, jealousy, greed, arrogance, resentment, inferiority, lies, and ego. The other is Good. It is joy, peace, love, hope, humility, kindness, empathy, and truth."

The grandson thought about this for a minute and asked his grandfather: "Which wolf wins?"

The wise man quietly replied, "The one you feed."

Native American proverb

To be sincere, is to reveal no thoughts.

The unspoken word is the truest prayer.

Be detached yet fully informed.

Proceed carefully,

while touching the world lightly.

Form is within emptiness and

Emptiness is within form.

Old Tibetan saying

As you are watching something from a distance,

simultaneously be aware that you too

are being observed.

Don't rattle that which you cannot cage.

Let the tiger destroy you,

do not resist and be empty enough

to discover that there is nothing to defend.

To be within your power you must not be looking for
recognition for what you have done.

When one is sincere, one realizes how much energy has

been lost and wasted.

When looking within,

do you discover yourself,

or find what you are looking for?

It's not what you believe that's important.

It's how you perceive what you believe.

When you are dissolved,

the heart will be in service.

To be or not to be is not the question.

To be who we are meant to be is the answer

and this requires feeling

what can't be tangibly assessed.

Here is where our journey truly begins.

Undo it by not doing it anymore.

Laughter is the breath

that emanates from one's heart.

The seer will receive every circumstance,

every human being within every encounter,

as an opportunity to learn about themselves.

www.parallelperception.com

To bee or not to bee, said the honey jar.

www.parallelperception.com

There is no thought.

There is only realization.

You are your home

and you are your environment.

Keep a clean house and let go of things

that are unnecessary.

www.parallelperception.com

We lag behind momentarily.

This is our condition:

To experience the moment continually escaping us.

We are existing as a memory.

Never forgetting is not really remembering.

The unknown enacts itself

in ways that are mysterious.

We have to apply trust in a way to prepare that the

world may harm us with anything,

so find safety within.

We must intend to raise our frequential essence to a vibration that is all encompassing in terms of the supportive effect that this will have upon humanity. We become one being. We start working together, not against each other.

We are here to devote to experiences and things that

we will eventually need to let go.

This is about cultivating 'no-thing'.

An awareness infused with silence

will listen to the rapture of the heart,

absorbing and expressing that feeling

as a conduit to the all-embracing mystery.

Accept the circumstances,

stand your ground and be who you are.

True power resides in not knowing where the next step
will be taken, for there lies one's irrefutable destiny, in
humble service to that which has not yet revealed itself.

Being of service is to do if you can,

and realize if you cannot.

www.parallelperception.com

Internal crisis from within will cause us

the inability to deal with crisis from outside.

An empath acknowledges what knocks upon their

being and acts instinctively in response

to that transmission from an alternate phylum that is

lovingly observing us.

This is the god consciousness that emerges

from the realm of antimatter,

which we are continually being born into

through its ethereal influence upon us.

Be a light unto yourself,

thus illuminating everything else.

Do not do or engage with anything

that you are ashamed of,

or that will break your integrity.

Be simple and plain.

Do not take possession of others.

Realize the experiences do not matter;

what is relevant is to remain still enough

to allow the mysterious to reveal itself.

Within the quietude of our breathing,

if we gently listen

to that which can't be heard,

we arrive upon our silence.

www.parallelperception.com

Everybody knows

what they do not want to face within.

Never work without a purpose.

www.parallelperception.com

The sacred geometry that exists

within an empath's heart

can translate into internal wisdom

if one's moment-to-moment recalibration

is pure enough to bear the consequence

of its' own expression.

Our feelings will always tell us if something is

appropriate or inappropriate.

www.parallelperception.com

When a bird awakes

upon the morning light, what does it do?

It sings with abandon.

One's limitation can also become one's strength.

Give of yourself

except for that which weakens you.

Accept what is given

but not that which compromises.

Always be aware of how much

possession possesses you.

To be somebody you have to be nobody,

and to be nobody gives you the ability to read

the feelings of your brother's and your sister's desires

within your own heart.

This is the way that we are meant

to function as symbiotic empaths.

Never take things for granted.

Within myself,

the other appears,

somewhere else.

What we need to know will be reflected

from each moment, just listen.

Do your practice and let life happen.

Not 'What if' or 'Maybe' but Reality.

Life can be a process of observing

what we are interfering with,

rather than interfering with

what we are observing.

One cannot possess what one wants to learn

but can only listen to what occurs.

Never betray yourself for social compliance.

How can you find your personal power

if you are blocked in emotion

instead of traveling upon the pure feeling

that you are meant to interpret?

And how can you have insights

if your mind gets in the way?

Beware of the destroyer within your power, always

stand your ground and be mindful

of the mirror that other people hold for you.

You never leave yourself

as an impression upon the world.

The world always leaves its

impression upon your silence.

This is how we travel,

upon this feather-light touch.

When you discover resistance,

just be humbled by it.

Watch, relax and allow it

to show you what needs to be seen.

The only path that has any meaning

is one that resolves your being

in the feeling that your heart is empowered

by doing what is necessary for your existence.

Be honest and speak truth.

We must remember that

the only true wealth we have

is the freedom of another human,

not their entrapment.

How can I know you

if I am not empty of myself?

Make your discipline stronger than your excuse.

Live a life that does not have an injured feeling.

The most profound state of awareness

comes from being devoted

to your present circumstances,

absorbing the sorrows and joys of others,

so that you may see yourself within them,

which in actuality is you.

www.parallelperception.com

Stillness within movement

and movement within stillness.

Be within your heart.

See and feel with your heart.

Recognize your heart within another.

Speak words from the heart.

Receive the words of another

within those precious chambers.

It is selfishness to focus on what we want

and not do what needs to be done.

The idea of enlightenment

is a cognitive bias.

In the end we are the sum total of our doings

and we will be faced by those doings

at the moment of our death.

Or is it our death in every moment that we live

that faces us with what we do?

Let go of who you think you are

and what you think you have achieved,

then the real achievement begins.

Things cannot be undone,

what was there and what was done,

leave it there.

What's important is now.

The quieter you become,

the more you are able to hear.

Lao Tzu

We are responsible.

There is nothing being done to us

apart from what we are doing to ourselves.

The more we become the less we increase.

The more we increase the less we become.

If a gesture is the most powerful command
that you have, then words mean very little.

To be underestimated and not be seen is good.

By not pronouncing you are something,

one learns to be nothing.

Withdrawal makes expansion possible.

In most cases, it's not what you do

but what you don't do

that delivers you

to a state of personal power.

There's nothing to be noticed

other than what's in front of us.

Don't even think about it.

Finding nothing

is to discover everything.

If you do not change direction,

you may end up where you are heading.

Lao Tzu

Stop being who you are not.

Do not linger. Lingering comes

from not knowing what to attach to.

As I am, so are others;

As others are, so am I.

Having thus identified self and others,

harm no one nor have them harmed.

Buddha

Nothing is unconscious.

You only have one chance,

and it lasts a lifetime.

As we get older, all we have

is the power of our body,

which also leads us

to the journey

of our

death.

Live Clean.

Stay Strong.

Do Your Practice.

Follow your sincerity.

At the center of your being

there is an answer.

Formlessness will create itself

from following a person's emptiness.

What we have become accustomed to witnessing is a

social illusion that takes precedence due to the fact that

the process is so intrusive

that it becomes difficult

to bear witness to the unobtrusive,

which is so subtle in comparison.

www.parallelperception.com

Do not let one's seeing ability

become an abuse of power.

Within myself the other appears,

somewhere else.

Trying is worthless, just do.

A crooked smile reveals a crooked path,

and a crooked mind that leans upon

a bent and crooked staff. From whence you came,

a crooked eye reveals its crooked aim,

the crooked wish to make you just the same.

Nothing to be said

but everything to be done.

Focus on your dreams.

Do not listen to the content
of expectations that may limit you.

Dream your heart forward.

Can you be trusted?

Within the silent reservoirs

of your own privacy, can you be seen?

In order to grow,

it is important not to judge.

To lose the opportunity

to truly be yourself

is a tragedy.

We need to let go

of our desire to be understood.

A tree will never tell you how strong it is

until you bump into it.

We are witnessing ourselves from all time.

Our thoughts and actions

echo throughout eternity;

They are noted and duly reflected back

upon ourselves.

No matter who we think we are,

we are never that person.

We are always the next being

who arrives upon our circumstance,

via their witnessing.

That is the truest individual you will ever meet; the one

you may encounter the next morning, who gazes upon

the sunrise

as they drink their tea by your side.

154

If we notice our circumstance,

we will always know what needs to be done.

We just need to forget ourselves

within that knowing.

Life will show you what you need to realize.

It is critical that we treat our life

as if we are at the end.

If we are act inappropriately,

we are actually killing

the moment we are still living in.

Never leave home without love.

Are we awake enough to be revealed

to the vision that is our life witnessing itself?

Self-regulation is more important than debate.

Allow people to be bathed in their own light.

Do not harm and pass negative

or poisonous energies onto others.

No gossip.

The path of enlightenment is only a foot wide

and a thousand miles deep,

and as you personally travel

towards your earnest realizations,

your sincerity will reveal the magnitude

of your responsibility as a human being.

To be truly free,

we have to stop being the past

and die to our old selves.

Never give up.

Life is suffering. Suffering demands service.

To be of service is to live with purpose.

And purpose is beautiful.

It brings elation. It brings courage.

It allows people to love you.

And you fall in love with life as a result

of your selfless and wholehearted engagement.

If you bring forth what is within you,

what you bring forth will save you.

If you do not bring forth what is within you, what you

do not bring forth will destroy you.

Yeshua

When a not-doing comes upon you,

and there is no reflection of yourself to be found, many

things can and will be related back to you as

knowledge. Yet you have no way of knowing how you

assimilated that wisdom.

Is it I who fear to die?

Or is it the dream

That fears I will expire?

One does things in harmony,

then harmony comes.

The best we can do in service to others

is to become the best of ourselves.

When listening to a person or situation,

look inward to discover how your heart feels.

This is the most profound state of communion.

Do not think you understand

and then move into defining things,

burn everything after use.

One is unable to see what's ahead

and still track the path behind.

We can only help ourselves

by stopping what we are doing

and focusing on the evolutionary process

that is continually escaping us.

We never know what we will become

and we are not supposed to know,

it can only be revealed when

that moment arises.

We need to realize that everything is a gift

and all gifts have to be received

in the present moment.

If you engage in your world with anything less than

purpose, you will be engulfed

by that which surrounds you.

Let go of what you know, to become realized.

To see more, you must become less.

Life can be a process of observing

what we are interfering with,

rather than interfering with

what we are observing.

There is nowhere to travel.

You are either here in your heart

or you are nowhere at all.

Internal wisdom primarily means the altering of one's

perception towards the ultimate truth:

A path with heart.

Adaptation without corruption

is the key to personal power.

Do not listen to one's internal dialogue,

for it is not pertinent to what is really happening.

Our hearts reveal our steps, even though

they are hidden from us and seen by others.

Or is it seen by us and hidden

until others realize?

Your prayer is your heart, whispering the truth which does not reveal itself through words.

When subtleties become substance,

wisdom arrives.

Let go of all your political opinions,

the only thing to do is dismantle

and release our own bias.

www.parallelperception.com

To genuinely be of service is to recognize

that life is composed of suffering.

And what a magnificent symphony it is.

Within this frequency, love will abound.

Action and inaction are the

true sides of the same coin.

There is no difference between relationship
and community, what matters is that
within those circumstances, you are you.

Touch softly that which cannot be touched. Gently

view that which cannot be seen.

Know that which cannot be known.

Step behind oneself,

don't think about what you are

supposed to do or not do,

let the circumstance inform you.

This is everybody's journey:

To be experienced and witnessed within the confines

of this frailty, which is our human body that moves

towards its inevitable end.

The only way to strengthen this frailty is to know

exactly who you are and do exactly what you know you

need to do. To claim your power this way is the only

worthwhile path to be undertaken as a human being.

If you forgive another

and they cannot forgive you,

then you have to leave,

or you will lose the capacity to truly be you.

Everything further develops and changes. Nothing is real except the moment that we arrive upon, which is continuously escaping us.

The illusion of suffering reflects back twofold through one's desire to be seen.

Know within yourself that time is limited

and to waste an ounce is a travesty.

To compress this valuable resource is essential, for to

squander time is to lose our life,

and when it is gone it cannot be retrieved.

To be waylaid is to

waste one's life and one's time.

When one understands it is not about 'me',

then one realizes it is about everything else, including

the programs that we need to face

as a collective and eventually overcome.

Constant renewal is the only internally vibrant point of

reference that we can truly recapitulate, via the fact that

we wait for it to manifest

as an arrival that has wisdom encased within it; instead

of a subjective injection that reflects one's wants and

needs, which may be socially bound to its own motive.

Focus on that inner beauty, that inner silence,

so that you may recapture yourself

and not be captured by something else.

The problem with human beings is that they think

they've got a choice.

We do not know what's part of our origin

and what destiny has in store for us.

We really cannot anticipate

what is waiting for us.

We can only try our very best

to minimize the holding patterns

and maximize truth in our life.

204

One's heart is our true temple

that permanently abides within.

Life is a constant meditation.

Work with nothing while one meditates

and work with something as things arise.

Thus, contemplate inwardly and outwardly.

If one walks it,

one does not need to talk it.

There is great magic in arriving and not understanding

yet remaining at one's center.

Everything we do has consequences.

How often do we or can we really understand

our own actions and their impact upon others?

Do we have the ability to know if we

are putting others in danger?

Embodying recapitulation as a practical application to

one's path means not living

the way you used to live and being so completely

in the moment that you are lost to yourself.

To give the best of oneself to every circumstance without background noise is to reside in not knowing; no position, no mind, just plain innocence and vulnerability.

Knowing oneself is a complex affair

wrapped in simplicity.

Split the wood, Lift the stone

and you will find me there.

Yeshua

Change will happen through

collective consciousness.

Attempt to change no one;

be that change.

When there's a brick wall in front of you,

what's important is to realize that there is

no brick wall in front of you.

To be mindful is not to follow the mind

but to be empty of that chatter.

Your journey is at hand

and you are responsible.

The Books of Lujan Matus

The unique teachings of Lujan Matus are a priceless resource of wisdom that pertain directly to human evolution. His responsibility to embody and transmit that legacy defines his purpose and is the driving force behind his work.

As a teacher and guide, Lujan offers tools and techniques that allow you to recognize and develop your own personal relationship with the unknown. He embraces the all-encompassing view of empathy and compassion as the essential foundation of his philosophical approach.

Complex yet practical, each edition builds upon the subtle framework defined by your own personal journey, in accordance with your life path. With each subsequent reading you will discover new aspects of your inner self and deepen your understanding of the very subtle application of empathic communion.

For information regarding workshops

and private tuition with Lujan Matus please visit:

www.parallelperception.com

Made in the USA
Monee, IL
12 February 2021